The Quest for Puma Poetry

Observing Nature
by Dayanara M., 3rd Grade

Bunny by Esmeralda G., 5th Grade

Table of Contents

Reading a Book
by Natalie C., 3rd Grade

Love by Angeles N., 5th Grade

Introduction

The Quest for Puma Poetry is a collection of poems by 4th and 5th graders from Mark Keppel School. It also includes some art pieces from 3rd to 5th grade students. Students began meeting for about 30 minutes, 3 to 4 times a week starting in August 2015. Most students knew very little about poetry and most had never written a poem before. Over the course of the year, students learned about how a poem is different than other forms of writing, image and sound devices, line and stanza breaks, how to analyze and read poetry, and even how to write and read their own work in front of the entire school.

Poetry is a special form of writing because it gives the writer permission to express themselves in unique and personal ways. It has been my deepest pleasure to watch these students grow into poets. The class has maintained great enthusiasm in spite of frequently being pushed out of their comfort zones. I watched students go from being terrified about reading in front of our classroom to reading without fault in front an audience of hundreds. Some have gone on to write poems independently and even began to identify themselves as poets.

The students made most of the decisions in creating this book, from its title, the cover art, and choosing the poetry. Thirty-six students each have three poems included in this collection. This book is ultimately their collaborative work of art.

Thanks is due to the 4th and 5th grade teachers for allowing me to keep stealing their students as often as I could. Special thanks is also due to Ms. Cantafio's 3rd grade class for supplying a huge chunk of the art. Finally, to Dr. Sanco for giving us permission to influence young minds in the art of poetry.

With much gratitude,
Ms. Tatro

By Isaac G., 5th Grade

Aaron V.
5th Grade

Where I'm From

I am from PS4
I am from bleach and couch
I am from the duplex
The rose and the birch tree
I am from reunion and playing cards
I am from soccer and baseball
I am form Alex and Leticia
From sports
I am from don't do drugs and never give up
I'm from the Jesus song
From celebrating Thanksgiving a weekend early
I am from Lynwood
I am from San Matías, Mexico
From tacos and shrimp
I'm from mom racing with grandpa's Mustang
From an uncle building a house in the hot sun
I am from pictures of my family
I'm from my grandma's house

Kai Died

Here lies Kai
Who never went outside
He only lived on video games
His whole family cried
He couldn't earn a dime
His family went inside his room
His eyes popped out and Kai had died

Recipe for a Monkey Taco

A monkey taco is easy to make all you do is simply take
1 piece of hair
1 stack of smashed avocado
Some bear meat
1 chicken leg
1 hard shell taco
1 monkey
1 banana
1 dash of salt
That has to do it
And now comes the problem
To tell the monkey to stop swinging

Abraham E.
4th Grade

Where I'm From

I am from a computer
From beds and toys
I am from a white house
That smells like roses
I am from the daisy
From the palm tree
I'm from singing and cooking
From Oscar and Maria
I'm from go eat Popeye's and go to the park
And from Las Vegas
I'm from never give up and keep going good
And La Cucaracha
I'm from partying
From Long Beach
I am from Mezcala
From tacos and pizza
I am from passed the border from Mexico
I am from my grandmother's necklace
In a safe in my mind

Ghost

I found myself a ghost
As scary as it could be
I'd thought I'd keep it as a pet
And let it play with me
I tried to wrestle and
Threw myself on it
But I slammed my face
On the floor, darn it!

The Dirty Dump

Here lies Rocky Fox,
Who went in a pile of stinky socks
Rocky turned green and
Got chicken pox
And then he died
In a slimy box

Alexza B.
4th Grade

Recipe for a Polar Bear Cupcake

A polar bear cupcake
is fine to make
all you do is take
a cup of flour
a cup of Silk Milk
a teaspoon of chocolate
three eggs
a white polar bear
and a dash of sprinkles.
Now the problem,
putting it in the oven.
No, it ran away!

Panther

A rushing black cat
It hunts in the darkest twilight
Proud and pride claw sharp

Coral

Colorful magical
Living growing gleaming
Glowing in the dark
Beautiful

Alizay B.
5th Grade

I Am From

I am from clothes and shoes
From iPhones and iPads
I am from my house smelling like sunflowers
I am from lemon trees in the garden
Avocado trees in my cousin's yard
I am from Christmas and Thanksgiving
From Maria and my brother Anthony
I am from cooking and dancing
At my aunt's house
I am from always be kind and never be scared
From ABCs
I am from quinceaneras
I am from Paramount
And from Mexico
Tamales and tres leches
I am from my aunt skydiving on her 23rd birthday
I am from pictures in the living room
And memories of my family in my heart

Birthdays

Cake, ice cream
Celebrating, opening presents
Birthday girl, blowing out candles, balloons, piñata
Eating food, singing Happy Birthdays, jumpers
Lots of candy, presents
Candles, family members

Friendship

Fight for you
Respect and understand you
Include you always
End of sorrow
Need you everyday
Dependable and trustworthy
Stand by you
Happy and honest
Inspired by you
Play until the sun goes down

Allysa C.
5th Grade

Halloween

Spooky, bloody
Screaming, scaring, moaning
Costumes, sweets, pumpkins, trick-or-treat
Running, exciting, creeping
Decorated, haunted
Family, lanterns

A Recipe for a Party Sundae

A party sundae is easy to make.
All you simply take is
Three purple helium balloons,
One whole cake,
Some ice cream,
A cup of sprinkles,
One cup of candy,
One whole party,
A dash of glitter,
That should do it.
And here comes the problem...
Finding a spoon big enough!

Where I'm From

I am from electronics
From soap and perfume
I am from the peach and tall apartments
Smell of blue flowers
I am from the palm tree
The rose bush
I am from family gatherings and celebrations
From Mariah and Ruby
I am from music, Connect Four
And family movie night
I am from work hards and love yous
And the ABCs
I'm from Día de los Muertos
I'm from Bellflower
And from Mexico
From tamales and mole
I'm from grandparents coming from El Salvador
From my grandpa's blind eye
I'm from taking pictures
And family mementos on my wall

Amber S.
4th Grade

Nanny

Here lies the body of Nanny
She had some maggot cheese
She thought they were little peas
She ate it and she fainted
And then she finally died the next week

My Tooth Fell Out

A tooth fell out, and left a space
So big my tongue can touch my face
And every time I smile
I show a space where something used to grow
I miss my tooth as you can guess
But then I have to brush one less!

Leprechaun

Why do they trick you?
Why are they small?
Why green? How about blue or violet?
Why do they steal money?
Why not chocolate, mud, or even cereal?

Argelia M.
5th Grade

Where I Am From

I am from pencils
From spoons and beds
I am from apartments
I am from hard smells

From roses in my room
I am from daisies just sitting there
From Christmas cheers and Thanksgiving
I am from Maria and Roberto

I am from Disneyland and the beach
I am from Spanish music
From being good to others and follow your heart

I am from the ABCs
From New Years
I am from Paramount
I am from Mexico

From tortas y tamales
I am from my sister
From the wedding my auntie had in church
From those pictures we took on the wall

Lemonade

I made myself a glass of lemonade
as sugary as can be
I needed to keep it as a pet
I let it sleep with me
I sewed it some pajamas
and a pillow for its head
Last night I decided to trade it for a candy
instead of having it as a pet

Love

Love is love until you find the one you love
Friends are friends until you find the one
That really cares about you
And love to me was nothing until the day I met you
So please love this poem, it's just for you

Aryanna M.
4th Grade

If Bubbles Were Bullets

If bubbles were bullets I'd take
a shot for you. If bubbles were
bullets I'd blow them out for you.
If bubbles were bullets I'd
pop them out for you.
If bubbles were bullets I'd do
anything for you.

The Regret Ride

Woosh!
Down it goes.
So fast it lasts one blink.

Screaming is the only sound.
All of a sudden! Screech!
A stop.

So high above the ground
It looks like the opening
To doors of Heaven.

But then, a slight move
And here we go on
Another ride.

Where I'm From

I am from coffee tables,
From pots and pans
I am from wooden floor
The smell of fresh cornbread
I am from the mini palm
The fresh lemon from the tree

I am from BBQ and talkative
From Ramon and Oscar
I'm from talking and stumbling
And from tripping
I'm from cleaning up and good job and over the river

I'm from giving gifts
I'm from Long Beach and Mexico
Burritos and enchiladas
From dad's broken ankle
That pine cone caused
Trip and pain

From that Christmas in El Aguaje
All of us together
That memory stands in my heart

Bernardo A.
5th Grade

Mummy

turn, turn
crash, crash
woosh, woosh
stop, stop
we're all
smelling dead people
mummy's saying
capture them
we're all getting
revenge and you
will die
people screaming
aaaaaaah hellllp
mummy king said
no escape no escape
woosh, woosh
boom, boom
we're all rushing
to get out
woosh, woosh
we survived
yaaaaaay
we all got out
the ride

Where I'm From

I am from video games
From soccer and dancing
I am from a pool apartment
And house smelling like strawberries
I am from roses
The 3 trees in front of my house
I'm from Christmas and Valentine's
From Ana and Angela
I'm from Hometown Buffet and Bianchi Theaters
And Las Vegas
I'm from to be the best and be a good son
And the ABC's song
I'm from New Years
I'm from California
And Mexico
From cheeseburgers and chicken tacos
I am from a ranch and family
From Luis
The celebration of my grandma's birthday
In my closet there is a picture
When my mom and dad met
I am from those moments

Zombie Sandwich

A zombie sandwich is easy really to make
All you do is simply take
One slice of bread
One slice of human brain
Some blood
One ripped arm
One zombie
One piece of string
A dash of salt
That ought to do it
And now comes the problem…
Tell that zombie I am not food

Briceida C.
5th Grade

Roger into a Goose

Here lies Roger
After seeing the Dodgers loose
He turned into a goose
He was shot down
And never found

Mummy Ride

the ride begun
I clenched on the grip
as strong as I could
ahhh!
fast fast
as the ride goes along
it was horrifying
zombie beside me
felt like it was bumping me off
it was gross as a monkey
it was terrifying

Where I Am From

I am from tables of food
From phones and hover boards
I am from sweet funny home full of joy
I am from smooth walls
And red fresh roses
I am from guava trees
I'm from soccer and helpful family
From Carlos and Esmeralda
From beach and amusement parks
I'm from go fishing
I'm from it's nice to be important
But important to be nice
And always smile no matter what
From everything its time
I'm from family movie night
From Paramount
From a Mexican ancestry
I'm from carne asada and pozole
From a cousin ditching school
From my smart and wise mom
From an emerald ring in my grandma's house
And always in my heart

Bryan G.
5th Grade

Piñata

I found myself a piñata,
As colorful as could be,
I thought I'd keep it as a pet,
And let it celebrate with me,
I made it a box for a bed,
And ice cream for a pillow,
Then last night it ran away,
But first, it forgot its guts,
The candy!
Yum!

The Bicycle Ride

Hands sweating as I gripped onto the handle bars,
In the middle of the road,
The cars beeping and honking,
As my cousin's scooter went "broom",
Then I looked up and I saw the finish line up ahead,
"Bump, bump" I went,
"Chirp, chirp" went a bird,
"Bark" went a dog,
"Hey" said my friend,
"Whoosh" I went,
As I won the race.

I Cannot Go to Work Today
inspired by I Cannot Go to School Today

"I cannot go to work today,"
Said Ms. Ann Olay,
My throat is dry,
I cannot see through my right eye,
I shall lie,
Till I die,
My temperature is 108,
I can't even open the front gate,
I must've have said a million "Ows"
Am I seeing cows,
I have blisters on my toes,
I can't even wear my favorite bows,
I have my favorite outfit,
That does not fit,
Because my big armpit,
There are bees,
On my knees,
I cannot hear,
This is my greatest fear...
Wait, what was that,
I am late,
For a date,
This is no time to die,
Good-bye.

Candy A.
4th Grade

Spring

Flowers, sunshine, blooming,
Sprouting, playing, beautiful sky in
Spring, brightness

About My Family

Marvelous at drawing art
Young and crazy

Fearless at anything
Ambitious to reach goals
Make things or bake cakes
Inspired, inspired, inspired
Love wild animals
You can do it

Where I'm From

I am from bunk beds with stars,
From carpeted floors and dark oak table
I am from the small house
And light brown feeling lonely
I am from a cherry bush,
And the lemon tree near my garage
I'm from watching movies in a movie theater
And from playing football
From Jessy and Heidi
I'm from playing Monopoly
And playing in my garden
From playing soccer
I'm from never giving up
And not everything is perfect
And to not say "I can't do it"
I'm from playing basketball together
I'm from Long Beach Hospital
I'm from parents from Liberty in Salvador,
From In-N-Out burgers and dark chocolate
From my grandpa who died, I never met him
And pictures of my family in my parent's closet

Darryl H.
5th Grade

Go Carts

The wind blowing in my face
WHOOSH WHOOSH
Racers drifting Errrrhhhh
Rubber burning in flames
Smoke filling the sky
Monstrous faces staring at me until
I win

First place

Football

Bloody Loud
Stretching Hitting Yelling
Helmet Players Pads Cleats
Running Coaching Autobowling
Complicated Dangerous
Teams Stickers

Where I'm From

I am from PS4
From hover boards and Ripsticks
I am from apartments
I am from sunflowers
I am from jamaica and
The maple trees
I'm from movie nights
And storytelling
From Melissa and Darryl Sr.
I'm from sports and cooking
I am from dreams and football
And keep your head up
I am from game nights
I'm from Long Beach
And from Honduras
I'm from panades and fry-jack
I'm from islands
And from dark colors
I am from speed boats
I am from hiding in the closet

Destiny E.
5th Grade

Fluffy Monkey

Here lies the body of a monkey
who was so funky
and like to eat munchies
and died because he was so stocky

My Favorite Things

Pools, water guns,
monkeys, noodle,
dance, puppies,
horses, poodles

Math, racing,
soda, pools,
high tops, hearts,
dogs, and school

Where I'm From

I am from TV's
from music and tile floors
I am from a rough and purple house
I am from roses and pinecone trees
I am from Christmas and Valentine's Day
from Debbie and Marvin
I am from stores from praying and movies
from I love you to go do your homework
I am from "He is Jealous for me"
from going to church and a hospital in Norwalk
I am from tacos and burritos
from a mom in a car crash
to metal in her arm
I am from pictures in an album book

Eduardo M.
5th Grade

Don't Wear Those Jeans

Here lies the body of a kid off fleek
who was wearing his dirty jeans for a week
He smelled his jeans while he was eating beans
He was special because he didn't shower with Pantene
He should have cleaned with watermelon,
but he died from the all awful smellin'.

The Cat and the Dog

The cat and the dog were talking
The dog said, "I like to bark."
The cat answered by saying, "I try that too."
The cat said, "I like to meow."
The dog said, "I try that too. "
The dog said, "I barely get out because
I am a house dog."
The cat said, "I never go out because
I jump on house furniture so I agree with you."
The cat said, "The thing I hate the most is that the
owners barely play with me."
The dog answered by saying, "I know how you feel.
They do that to me too."

Where I'm From

I am from hard floor
From phones and technology
I am from the glass floor in my apartment
(Smells like roses)
I am from the white flowers
The yellow daisies
I'm from celebrating Christmas on Christmas Eve
And from posadas
From Juana and Roque
I'm from going to the mall
And traveling to family members' houses
From heading to church on Sunday
I'm from dream big and the three kings are real
From don't fight
I'm from going to church on the day of the Virgin Mary
I'm from Paramount
I'm from León, Mexico
I'm from tamales and carne asada
From my dad's father
They're both wise
The picture of the day my parents got married
I'm from shelves inside closets
From a great and pleasant family

Erika I.
5th Grade

Recipe For A Rhino Sundae

It's so simple to do
A Rhino Sundae
You just need

An enormous bowl of ice cream
Some strawberries,
Whip cream,
sprinkles,
A piece of string,
And one rhino

Believe me, that will have to do it
Now here comes the tough part
Scooping into it

Christmas

Cheerful Love
Exciting Amazing Enchanting
Family Santa Mistletoe Tree
Dancing Playing Eating
Colorful Massive
Decorations Toys

Where I Am From

I am from an iPad
From paintbrushes and t-shirts
I am from kind of small
I am from apartments that smell wonderful
The colorful flowers and many trees

I am from making big deals of birthdays
And having fun
From Eric and Luz
I am from talking and playing
And from watching "El Chavo"

I am from always say thank you
And follow your heart
And don't talk to strangers
I am from get together on Christmas
I am from Long Beach, CA
And Acapulco, Mexico

I am from enchiladas and burgers
From a brother who is greedy
who doesn't share his toys
From countless dazzling family pictures
On my wall

Esmeralda G.
5th Grade

Where I'm From

I am from shoes
From clothes and toys
I am from the white doors
Fresh air and calm
The guayaba tree

I am from celebrating Christmas and eating as a family
From Jorge and Adriana
I am from traveling and church
And from spending time together

I am from I love you and stay close to me
And don't talk to strangers
I am from celebrating a holiday with all my family
I am from Bellflower
From Mexico
Tamales and menudo
From trouble making cousins
And curly hair
I am from trips to Knott's Berry Farm
And from pictures in the photo album

Bunny

Brown and white bodies
Hopping up and down around
Munching up carrots

Christmas

Joyful traditional
Singing decorating hugging
Presents tree stockings ginger bread
Smiling eating dancing
Giant colorful
Bells food

Fabiola M.
5th Grade

Fastest Ride

It was about to start
I held on tight, the ride
Went faster and faster
The screams were heard louder
And louder from hearing
All the screaming I wished
I was just dreaming, I
Shook in fear and once it
Was over it was a scary feeling
But also very thrilling

I Will Not

I will not clean my room
I'd rather play basketball
Where everyone is happy
And never cleans up
Where everyone scores
And never gives up
Where they're never that sad
But always have fun

Where I'm From

I am from an old TV
From tablespoons and clean towels
I am from the big house I live in
With the smell of grass
I am from sweet daisies
The old trees waving

I am from Thanksgiving and Easter
From Elvia and Maria
I am from cleaning and going on walks
From watching TV
I am from behave good and pay attention
And ABCs

I am from Christmas
From Paramount
And Mexico
I am from enchiladas and tamales
From the job my uncle lost
And the happiness of my sisters

I am from pictures in my book
From moments I'll never forget

Gabriel U.
4th Grade

Where I'm From

I am from park
I am from a two story house
I am from a high school across the street
I am from a skate park next to my house
I am from sports
I am from movies and games

I am from snowboarding
I am from never give up and don't get bullied
I am from taco and pozole
I am from Christmas and presents

I am from going to church
I am from a first communion
I am from Next Takeover

Brush Your Teeth

Here lies the kid who cries
he went to the dentist and he lies
The guy took out a tool
he died by being a fool

Family

My family always stood up for me.
They are at least the best thing that I will ever have.
They are my protection.
They take me everywhere I want to go.
If I get lost, they would do anything to find me.

Isaac G.
5th Grade

Jurassic Park

Dinosaurs roaring
The gate behind closing
Up, up, up
Until it went dark
Through the wall
You could see the whole park
1, 2, 3, 4, 5... BOOM!!
Zooming
At the speed of light
Screams could be heard
SPLASH!!
It had ended
We all laughed.

Frog in My Closet

There's a frog in my closet
He jumped in my sweater pocket
I put it on last week but took it off with a shriek
It jumped out the door
But I think he came back
And made a mess on the floor

Where I'm From

I am from soap, tablets, and Xbox One
From bright green grass
From the neighborhood block
I'm from roses
From the tree in front of our house
I am from Christmas and Halloween
From Valery and Cesar
I am from barbeques and soccer
From church
From I will succeed and good job
And treat others how you want to be treated
I am from camping in the great outdoors
From Lynwood
I'm from Honduras
From turkey sandwiches and carne asada
From Karla
Always happy
All in my closet

Jacob M.
5th Grade

Recipe for a Deer Waffle

A deer waffle is quite the dish,
And all you need is:
2 toasters,
2 pounds of wheat,
Your state quiz,
4 empty water bottles,
A deer,
Some video games,
And then you blend it.
But there is a problem...
There is not enough space in the blender!

My Favorite Things

Star Wars, Playstation,
Movies, mango.
Pizza, ice cream,
TV, Nintendo.
Lightsabers, phones,
And French toast.
These are things
I like the most.

Star Wars

A long time ago in a galaxy far far away
Shooting, dueling, speeding
Lightsabers, Darth Vader, Luke Skywalker, blasters
Flying, spying, mind-tricking
Powerful, Sci-fi
Death Star, planets

Jordan M.
5th Grade

Punch O' War

I will not play tug o' war
I'd rather play punch o' war
where everyone punches
And where everyone bleeds
And where people faint and where
Everyone screams and everyone
Cries and when everyone dies
But one survies

Wild Leopards

They have dangerous speed
They scratch bite they kill
But also they protect their
family.

Where I Am From

I am from FIFA 16, PS3
I am from soccer and football
I am from a big house and 3 rooms
I am from dinner
I am from roses and dandelions
I am from jalapenos that my grandma planted
I am from my dad, Salvador, and my mom, Veronica
 that took care of me when I was little
I am from surprises and wishing
I am from a park for soccer practice
I am from normal songs and oldies songs
I am form Christmas and baby Jesus
I am from Paramount and Somerset Blvd
I am from Mexico
I am from tamales and pozole
I am from my brother that breaks walls
I am from cousin that is very smart
I am from my backpack
I am from my closet when my parents were together

Katelyn S.
4th Grade

Roller Coaster

Crook crook
Screams
Up up

Pause

Wind blowing
Whoosh hands
Going into the air

Down then
Drop in the safe zone

Summer

sunny days
swimming relaxing traveling
beautiful weather in summer
brightness

Where I'm From

I am from an iPod
From picture frames and wooden tables
I am from kind of big
I am from roses
And palm trees
I'm from inviting family members to my house
And from having parties
From mom and dad
I'm from playing board games and going on trips
Together and from going on bike rides
I'm am from I love you and never give up
And don't talk to strangers
I'm from getting together on holidays
I'm from Paramount, CA and from Ensenada
I am from tamales and pozole
From never meeting my grandpa
From mom's side
I'm from pictures from the past
Under my bed

Kenyea C.
5th Grade

Feather Death

Here lies the body of Heather
She didn't do nothing but ate a feather
The feather she ate choked her to death
Then she took her last breath

Lions

Golden winter fur
So soft so fury and brave
Fierce roar big mane

Where I'm From

I am from Madden 25,
from dogs and movies.
I am from the blue paint in my room
smells like dinner.
I am from rose petals
the sweet oranges from our orange tree.
I am from barbecuing and basketball,
from Marcello and Jordan.

I am from cursing and playing football,
from eating at buffets.
I am from business before pleasure
and don't ever give up.
I am from Trap Queen,
from being aggressive.

I am from Paramount,
from mac and cheese and cornbread.
I am from a grandmother that throws glass bottles,
and people getting cut by small glass pieces.
I'm from my family portrait,
from the closet where I keep funeral clothes
and my favorite book, *Winnie the Pooh*.

Kimberly R.
5th Grade

Friend Poem

Friendly and kind
Respectful and honest
Incredible also awesome
Excellent
Never lies
Does not fight

Basketball

athletic, agile
bounding, shooting, blocking
court, three-pointer, free shot, net
running, jumping, screaming
tireless, terrific

Where I Am From

I am from clothes
From books and pillows
I am from kind of small
Calm
I am from roses
Tulips
I am from family time and praying together
From Yadira and Mario
I am from movie night and picnic
Playing board games.
I am from I love you and always try your best
From my baby girl
I am from celebrating Easter
I am from Cerritos
From Mexico
Pozole and ceviche
I am from my grandpa cut his hand
He had to get stitches
I am from pictures when I was a baby
In a heart

Leslie C.
5th Grade

The Magical Pegasus

one day I saw a Pegasus
it was making rainbows
so I thought I should take it home,
I made it a bed, pillows, and blankets,
the next day I took it out for a walk
but then whoosh!!
it flew away making rainbow trails

R.I.P. Larry Say

Here lies the body of Larry Say
Who wore the same socks every day
People passed out as he walked in the hallway
His feet smelled like a dead possum
That wasn't very awesome
He smelled his feet and fell asleep
Forever

Where I'm From

I am from TV
From couches and coffee tables
I am from a white house
From roses
I am from orange trees
And from flowers
I am from birthdays and holidays
And from Adriana and Ricardo
I am from dinner as a family
And from amusement parks
I am from Santa Claus
And from church songs
I am from Torrance Hospital
And from go to church
And from Mexico
I am from strawberries and chicken enchiladas
I am from cousins
And from funny personalities
I am from pictures of family
And from memories in a photo album

Lisa R.
5th Grade

The Walking Dead

Pitch Black   Bloody Red
Running   Yelling   Stopping
Prison   Zombies   Cars Food
Limping   Bleeding   Hiding
Rotten Scary
People   Ammo

Our Stars

Our stars shine bright for us,
Up in the night.
But we can't see them,
Because of the city lights.
We cry and cry for the stars to appear,
Then one night the stars are clear.

Where I'm From

I am from needles,
From chairs and windows,
I am from the flowers growing in the yard.
I am from the food I smell as I walk in.
I am from the white roses and the peach tree.

I'm from brunettes and curly hairs
From Musset and Freddy.
I'm from reading and watching,
From playing sports.
I'm from staying quiet and being respectful.
I'm from Hush Little Baby,
From Easter.
I'm from Paramount,
From Phoenix, Arizona.
I am from tortas and asopes.
From my father hurting his arm at work,
His cut healed.

I am from pictures hidden behind a shelf.

Luis A.
5th Grade

Where I Am From

I am from skateboards
From Xbox One and stoves
I am from an orange house
I am from always smelling like food
I am from the guava tree
From roses beside my window
From being together and watching TV
I am from uncles and aunts
I am from soccer and football
From playing board games
I am from work hard and be good
From Día de los Muertas
I am from Bellflower
From Paramount and Mexico
I am from carne asada and tacos
I am from large scars on my uncle's hand
From my brother's scooter accident
I am from photos of my childhood
In a box in the attic

Funny Moments on a Roller Coaster

click click
screaming
it felt like I was dreaming
it was high
I was scared
and I'm a guy
I was all the way
in the sky
I told my sister
I wasn't scared but I lied
this might
be boring
but it's my story
I thought it was over
but I was still on
I thought I was goner
but now I am older
I thought it was worth money
it was so sunny
I was hungry
for my tummy.

Little Old Man

There was a man
That was as short as a kid
There was a short kid
They met on the sidewalk
They started to talk
The kid was crying 'cause of his height
And the guy said why are you crying
The kid knew not to talk to strangers
The kid said 'cause of my height
And the guy said don't worry
Anyway we're alike

Matthew R.
4th Grade

Where I'm From

I am from a coffee table
From the oil in the cabinet
From love in the air
I am from a tiled floor
From the brush in the cabinet
I'm from the white rose bush outside my window
I am from a banana tree outside my house

I am from loving and caring
I'm from Rusha and Obar
From arguing and playing video games
I am from going walking
From love you at arm's length
And never get bit twice
I'm from live to the fullest

From family dinners
I am from hospital
I'm from Texas
From mac and cheese and fried chicken
I am from the time I made it out alive
And the cane on the floor
From the basement mural

I'm from a ring on a precious finger

Legend of the Kraken

Kraken
cyan, magenta
swimming, splashing, emerging
boat, storm, tentacles, legend
dashing, killing, horrifying
hunted, scary
ark, tornado

Snake Lemonade

Snake lemonade is easy to make
all you do is simply take
one glass of ice
one snake
a bite of venom
a bit of slime
one lemon
a bit of sugar too
that ought to do it
now here comes the problem
having the snake
not slither away

Nalleli V.
5th Grade

Where I'm from

I am from books and electronics
From large windows in my living room
I am from the smooth walls
I am from the chili bush from the loquat tree
I am from Mother's Day and same blood
From Arely and Stephanie
I am from camping and Sunday reunions
And going to the beach
I'm from defending and be kind
I am from think of others,
From Father's Day dance
I'm from Suburban Hospital
And from Mexico, San Antonio, Guaracha
I'm from tamales all the way to enchiladas
I'm from my dad broke his arm
And from his bone that popped out
I am from his grandparent pictures
From them being on the wall and in our heart
Where I'm from is the real and best made world

Hit the Quan

I will not play hit the ball
But I will play Hit the Quan
Where everyone hits the quan not the ball
where everyone dances not runs around
where everyone uses their hands and feet not a bat
where everyone swings their arms around not forward
But wait don't leave from here
first I'm going to show you how to
HIT THE QUAN
HIT THE QUAN
HIT THE QUAN

Jacob Sartorius

Jelly beans his favorite snack
Awesome at musical.ly
Cute with braces and eyes
Outside boy playing baseball
Best at "musical.ly" videos

Soccer his favorite sport
Airplane ride to Florida
Radical at his jokes
Top phone and phone case
Outstanding music videos
Rapper with videos in YouTube
Inaccurate and funny pics
Understandable writing and thoughts
Such an adorable and cute boy

Paula G.
5th Grade

Where I'm From

I am from dishes
From tables and chairs
I am from the white walls
Smelling like flowers
From the apple tree
I'm from Christmas and making tamales
From Jesus and Jovita
I'm from cleaning and church
And from praying together
I'm from I love you and stay here
And the alphabet
I'm from celebrating holidays with my family
I'm from Bellflower
From Mexico
I'm from enchiladas and tacos
From the finger my dad cut
He had to get stitches
From a picture at Disneyland
Under my bed

Puppies

brown and furry bodies
soft, cuddly, and adorable
loudly, playful, cute

Christmas

Happiness huge
Playing singing decorating
Bells dinner tree and presents
Hugging eating and dancing
Memorable colorful
Lights candles

Rhyeonna R.
5th Grade

Christmas

Colorful Careful
Hugging Dancing Playing
Family Lights Story Activities
Stocking Walking Singing
Happy Fun
Balls Food

Halloween

Spooky Scary
Screaming Crying Scattering
Walking Running Playing
Eating Knocking Ringing the bell
Family Haunted
Dream Lights

Where I'm From

I am from California
From TV and clothing
I live in an apartment
It tastes like food
I am from the trees
With rose flowers
I am from music and dancing
From Malina and Brandon
I am from listening to hip-hop and playing Monopoly
From watching Criminal Minds
I am from how to be nice and how to be myself
From learning a song
I am from going to church
From Paramount
I am from living in the city
From mashed potatoes and chicken
I am from getting a red eye
From taking a picture

Samantha S.
4th Grade

Butterfly

Fluttering in the sky
The beautiful patterns
On their wings

Staying still for it to
Land who knows
Where it will go
Maybe Disneyland or
Maybe In-N-Out to get

A burger seeing the
Patterns so hard to
Catch maybe next
Time

Ice Cream

Cold and refreshing
Useful for hot summer
Days so many flavors

Which shall I choose
Explosion of flavors
Melts strawberry, chocolate, and
Vanilla 1 scoop or 3 scoops or maybe a
Cherry to top it all off

Unicorn

Are they real or
Evil or lovely as can be
Flying or not crying or
Not enchanted hair

Barfing rainbows sweet
Or puke, I just really want a
Pet unicorn

Vanessa B.
5th Grade

Crying

crying,
everyone does it,
maybe getting a new pet,
or seeing a family member from the military,
or even seeing a family member dying,
or knowing that the thing you want so badly
won't ever happen,
or even crying because you broke your arm,
or even from watching a scary movie,
or even crying because a friendship ended,
or even from getting denied from a job,
no matter what you're crying from
madness, sadness, excitement, or fear
you cried since the day you were born

Ocean

blue, sparkly
calming, swaying, swooshing, roaring
reflecting in the sunlight

Best Friend

Believe in you
Encourage you
Stand by you
Tell you stories

Forget about the arguments
Respect you
Inspire you
Everlasting laughing
Never spread rumors
Determine if you should move on

Vianey V.
4th Grade

Where I'm From

I am from bobby pins
From glowing stars and floating lamps
I am from the sweet smell of my mom's cooking
Smells like corn masa
I am from roses
Lemon trees oranges
I am from quiceneras and Day of the Dead
From a brother and 2 sisters
I am from painting and coloring and playing
I am from treating others the way I want to be treated
And not talking to strangers
From Twinkle Twinkle Little Star
I am from cutting the bread
And retrieving the baby made of jelly
I am from Compton
From Guadalajara
From carne asada and tamales
I am from my mom riding a horse across the farm
And into the future
I am from pictures on the walls
In the closet
In my shoebox in my heart

Flower Pot

Fragrantly beautiful
Lovely
Outstanding plants
With
Encouraging colors
Recognizing

People who've
Outgrown them yet
They still find the time to stay a flowerpot

Mythology

powerful caring
demanding helping willing
warriors thieves killers hero
fighting creeping crawling
inconsiderate fearless
goods goodness

Victor M.
5th Grade

The Arty and Marty Fart

Hear lies the body of Arty
He was playing with his friend Marty
They both had a party
Then the next day they both died from being too farty

Scarecrow

I made myself a scarecrow
as scary it could be
I thought
I'd keep it as a friend
to let it stay with me
I made the scarecrow
a bed and some blankets too
and every time in the morning
I forget it's there and
I always get scared

Where I'm From

I am from TV
From PS4 and MLB the Show
I am one story house with a pool
Feel all the holidays at my house
I am sunflowers
The avocado tree
I am from Christmas and Valentines
From Angelica and Victor
I am from baseball tournaments
And Life, the board game
From Dodgers and Lakers games
I am from try your best and never give up
And from "Hall of Fame" the song
I am from Long Beach
I am from Mexico
From tacos and tamales
From my uncle Saul that never gave up in UCLA
From grandpa that passed away
And got his scarf, hat, and favorite sun glasses
From on my shelf so I can remember him

Playing with Colors and Form
by Ashley A., 3rd Grade

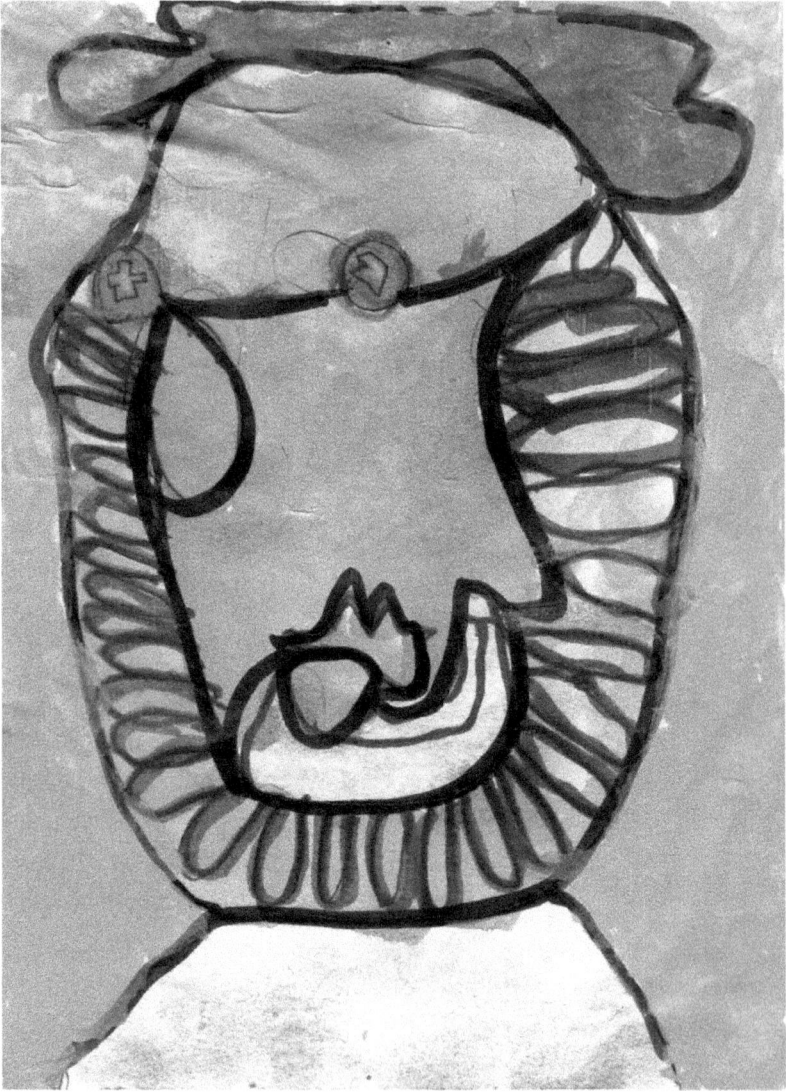

The Man Looking at the Mirror
by Ramiro G., 3rd Grade

Student Bios

Aaron V. is a 5th grader who likes to play soccer, and loves eating chocolate. He is the middle child, and his favorite color is blue.

Abraham E. lives in Paramount, is in 4th grade, and goes to Mark Keppel. He likes to play soccer and he likes donuts.

Alexza B. is a 4th grader who goes to Mark Keppel, loves technology, loves to dance, and Chick Fillet.

Alizay B. loves family and friends, is a 5th grader, and her favorite color is purple.

Allysa C. likes running and reading, also likes to play on her tablet, and likes Starbucks, and also, Cristiano Ronaldo.

Amber S. loves drawing, eats healthy, has a lot of friends, loves nature and draws flowers.

Argelia M. is a 5th grader who lives in an apartment, loves hanging out with her friends, really loves music, and she loves playing her iPad.

Aryanna M. is a 4th grader at Mark Keppel, loves origami, chocolate, and bacon.

Bernardo A. likes to go to Mark Keppel Elementary School. He likes to play soccer and write poems. His teacher's is name Ms. Tatro; she teaches him about poetry.

Briceida C. loves puppies, likes to eat junk food, although she is smart. She likes to go to Disneyland, likes math, and likes to go for walks on the Santa Monica Pier.

Bryan G. is a 5th grade boy who likes soccer and drawing and his favorite subject is math.

Candy A. is 4th grader who goes to Mark Keppel, and loves strawberry with chocolate.

Darryl H. likes sports and cares about his family. He likes to eat, he doesn't like books, and he likes games.

Destiny E. is a 5th grader who loves math, is a dog lover, lives in Paramount, and loves to wear to Converse.

Eduardo M. likes soccer, is a student at Mark Keppel School and a 5th grade boy. He also lives in Paramount.

Erika I. is in 5th grade. She loves to sing, dance, read, her family, her friends, and art.

Esmeralda G. is a 10 year old in 5th grade who loves to sing and enjoys eating candy.

Fabiola M. is nice. She goes to Mark Keppel, likes to listen to music and she likes chocolate. She also loves money and flowers.

Gabriel U. is a 4th grader from Paramount. He likes tacos and most of all he likes sports.

Isaac G. likes to draw, play Xbox, play soccer, play handball, and likes Star Wars.

Jacob is a 10-year old boy in 5th grade who enjoys books, playing his Play Station 4, lives in Lakewood, CA, likes soccer and baseball, and loves cooking.

Jordan M. is in 5th grade at Mark Keppel. He plays soccer. He is great; also he is not that great at school.

Katelyn S. is in fourth grade. She loves to read and have fun. The most important thing to her is her family.

Kenyea C. likes to play football, soccer, and basketball; he also likes to play with electronics.

Kimberly R. is a 10 year old girl in 5th grade and likes singing and playing basketball. She also loves to eat chocolate.

Leslie C. is a 5th grader and from a family of five. She loves to hang with her family & friends, and she is 11 years old.

Lisa R. is a fifth grader who enjoys football and art, but also loves board games. She also loves animals and helping people.

Luis A. is a 5th grader who likes sleeping. He also likes playing video games. He's good at it. He likes playing with his friends.

Matthew R. is a creative, humble, hysterical, loving artist in 4th grader at Mark Keppel.

Nalleli V. likes to play soccer, read books, draw animals, have fun, go camping, do traditions in my family, go to my cousins' houses, and most of all write poems. That's why she has become a poet.

Paula G. is a 5th grader at Mark Keppel School; she likes to spend time with her family and friends.

Rhyeonna R. loves drawing flowers and going to the beach, shoes and playing.

Samantha S. is a 4th grader who loves chocolate, strawberries, and raspberries, also likes dance.

Vanessa B. loves dogs and Olive Garden, enjoys going to the beach and dreams to be a successful in life.

Vianey V. is a 4th grader who loves reading books, eating fruit, beautiful dresses, the color turquois, and school.

Victor M. is a 5th grader, who is good at math, likes basketball, is awesome at baseball, and is a 10 year old boy.

The Man in Blue
by Keven M., 3rd Grade

I Love Poems Too
by Gerardo C., 5th Grade

www.ingramcontent.com/pod-product-compliance
Lightning Source LLC
Chambersburg PA
CBHW060339050426
42449CB00011B/2792